To Mom in the hospital
Nov. 4, 1993
from
Laurie & Gary
& family

Loving One Another

Loving One Another

Alice Joyce Davidson

Fleming H. Revell Company
Old Tappan, New Jersey

Davidson, Alice Joyce.
    Loving one another.

    1. Religious poetry, American.   I. Title.
PS3554.A922L6   1984   811'.54   83-16145
ISBN 0-8007-1388-5

Scripture quotations in this book are taken from the King James Version of the Bible.

The twelve poems in "Through the Year" by Alice Joyce Davidson are from DAILY GUIDEPOSTS, 1983. Copyright © 1982 by Guideposts Associates, Inc., Carmel, New York 10512. Reprinted by permission. All rights reserved.

Dedicated to the children,
mine and yours,
with a prayer for a
peace-filled tomorrow

CONTENTS

Dear Friends,
Let us love one another . . . by sharing
needs, by thoughtful deeds, by spreading
hope and cheer . . . and through all seasons of
our lives, may God be very near.

Lovingly and prayerfully,

Alice Joyce Davidson

1
The Ways of Love

Deep Within

There is
within each one of us
a bit of God above . . .
for in each life,
God breathed a soul,
and in each soul
breathed love.

Hereby know we that we dwell in him, and he in us, because he hath given us of his Spirit.

1 John 4:13

Eternal Love

Come,
my love,
and let us lift up
our eyes to the heavens . . .

let us open wide
the doors of our hearts
to God . . .

for love
that is rooted in faith
is eternal!

. . . let them also that love thy name be joyful in thee.

Psalms 5:11

"... Love One Another ..."

Three little words—
  but they can bring
    the rainbow after rain
And chase away
  the clouds that cause
    sorrow, ache, and pain!

Three little words—
  but they can turn
    a foe into a friend,
Break the walls of hate
  and cause
    intolerance to end!

Three little words—
  but they can set
    the world on course, and then
Bring understanding
  and goodwill
    to humankind again!

Three little words
  the Lord gave us—
    dear sister and dear brother,
Let's join our hearts,
  let's join our hands
    LOVING ONE ANOTHER!

**Beloved, let us love one another: for love is of God; and
every one that loveth is born of God, and knoweth God.**

1 John 4:7

Your Love Comes to Me

In so many ways Your love comes to me—
Feelings to cherish, treasures to see . . .
On so many days my heart fills with cheer
Feeling Your presence, the glow of You near . . .
Your love comes to hold me, enfold me with care
Whenever I'm troubled or filled with despair . . .
Your love comes to me when I need guidance, too,
And You show me the way to abide close to You . . .
As countless as stars or waves in the sea,
In so many ways Your love comes to me!

**How excellent is thy lovingkindness, O God! therefore the children
of men put their trust under the shadow of thy wings.**

Psalms 36:7

Give Me a Simple Task

I come before you, Lord, and humbly ask
Do you have work, a job you'd like to fill?
It needn't be a complicated task,
A simple deed will nicely fit the bill—
A door to hold while others pass on through,
A smile to make a stranger feel at ease,
An ear to lend a friend who's feeling blue,
Some time to share some golden memories,
A few crumbs tossed to feed the hungry birds,
A note to write that uplifts with its words—
Please keep me working, keep me working, Lord,
And fill my waking hours every day
With simple tasks well done . . . and my reward
Will be to know I'm walking in Your way!

Serve the Lord with gladness . . .

Psalms 100:2

Reach Out With Love

Let's shrink this world
   and make it cozier,
Let's make life bright,
   our future rosier,
Let's try to understand
   each other
As a sister
   or a brother,
Let's model earth
   after heaven above,
Let's all reach out—
   reach out with love!

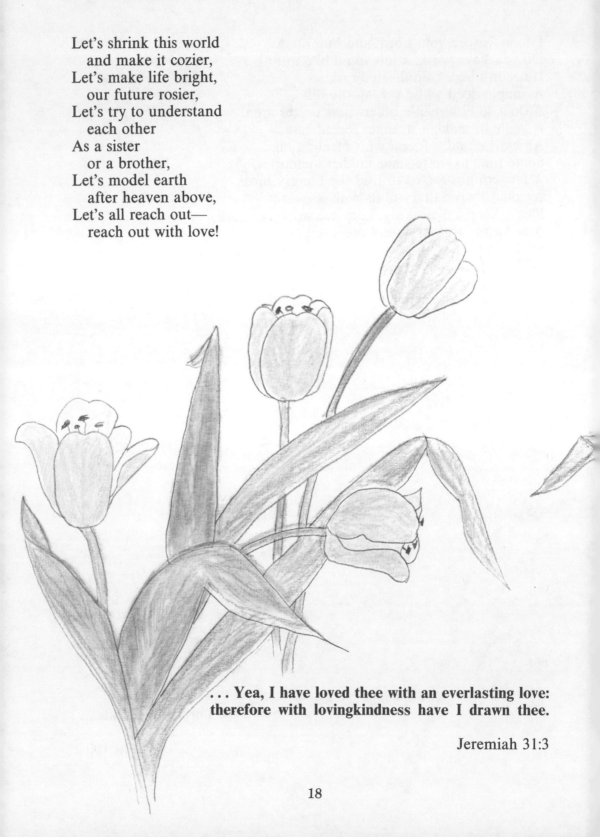

. . . Yea, I have loved thee with an everlasting love:
therefore with lovingkindness have I drawn thee.

Jeremiah 31:3

Closer Still

May the light of God surround us
So we may see His way.

May His might be all around us
And protect us day by day.

May His wisdom come into our hearts
So we may know His will.

May the love of God flow through us
And bind us closer still.

The Lord is good to all: and his tender mercies are over all his works.

Psalms 145:9

Blessed Stem

What am I, Lord?
A leaf in a storm,
being blown hither and yon
by the changing winds
of life?

No!
I am a leaf
on Your tree of life,
fastened to You
with a stem
of love!

**And thou shalt love the Lord thy God with
all thine heart, and with all thy soul, and
with all thy might.**

Deuteronomy 6:5

Planting Time

Take time to do a deed today,
To shoulder someone's load,
Take time to fill a need today
And smooth a rocky road . . .
Take time to plant a seed today
In the vineyard of the Lord,
And what you plant will yield for you
A wonderful reward!

. . . he which soweth bountifully shall reap also bountifully.

2 Corinthians 9:6

Fragile Flower

Love is a flower
that springs forth
from the warmth of caring,
and grows more beautiful
when it is nurtured
by two.

And once it is grown,
love survives the scorch of summer
as well as the cold fury of winter.

Only when it is saturated
by the waters of bitter salt tears,
does love fold up its flower head
and wilt.

Behold, thou art fair, my love . . .

The Song of Solomon 1:15

Love—A Little Word That Grows

Love,
it's such a little word
and yet it has great powers,
It seeps into our dreams and hopes
and fills our waking hours . . .

Love,
it's a balm that keeps us calm,
a heaven-on-earth touch,
A lift we feel, a gift we give
that means so very much . . .

Love,
it's a need we fill, a deed we do
filled with tender caring,
a little word that grows and grows
still better for the sharing!

. . . If we love one another, God dwelleth in us . . .

1 John 4:12

In His Image

God made us
in His own image,
which is why we find
our greatest purpose
in creating,
our greatest satisfactions
in giving,
our greatest happiness
in loving.

And God said, Let us make man in our image, after our likeness . . .

Genesis 1:26

Good Intentions

Don't let a good intention wait
Until another day,
Don't save a smile, or leave unsaid
The things you want to say . . .

For life is short and precious,
Golden moments are too few,
And the love you give to others
Will bring blessings back to you!

**Commit thy works unto the Lord, and thy thoughts
shall be established.**

Proverbs 16:3

Lo and Behold!

Awesome
is Your creative power.
Wondrous
are Your creations.

Out of darkness
You brought light!
Out of chaos
You brought matter!
Out of matter
You brought life!

Life! Matter! Light!
You created, Lord,
and are creating still!

Inexhaustible
is Your creative power!
Unfailing
is Your love!

. . . let all the inhabitants of the world stand in awe of him.

Psalms 33:8

26

A Second Look

You can't always tell the contents
From the cover of a book,
And people, too, cannot be judged
Without a second look . . .

Things aren't always as they seem—
An unfriendly frown might hide
A heartache or a feeling
Someone's yearning for inside . . .

Look past external things you see,
Seek out another's heart,
And often you'll find fertile ground
Where seeds of friendship start.

. . . for the Lord seeth not as man seeth; for man looketh on the outward appearance, but the Lord looketh on the heart.

1 Samuel 16:7

Just a Little Daisy

I have a little daisy plant
That brightens up my yard,
And through the years, I've come to hold
That plant in high regard . . .
I've used its perky blossoms
In numerous bouquets—
For Mother's Day, for weddings,
And to brighten sickbed days. . . .
My little plant has mothered plants
throughout the neighborhood,
And like myself, my neighbors
Have used their plants for good . . .
And I've learned a little lesson
From my daisy—for I know
The more I give to others,
The more I bloom and grow!

The earth, O Lord, is full of thy mercy . . .

Psalms 119:64

Greatness

Money, fame, and fortune
do not make for greatness—
greatness comes not from acclaim
but from the way we live.

Greatness comes from high ideals,
from quiet deeds we do,
from dreams we dream, from dreams we share,
from happiness we give!

Give, and it shall be given unto you . . .

Luke 6:38

2
Special Times and Special People

The Art of Living

Some people know
    a special art
Of living fully
    from the heart . . .
They soothe, they lift,
    they scatter cheer,
And you feel blessed
    when they are near.

. . . the path of the just is as the shining light . . .

Proverbs 4:18

Honoring Each Other

There's a day to honor mothers,
A day to honor fathers,
And grandparents, too, now have a special day . . .

Let us honor all our cousins,
Our sisters and our brothers,
And neighbors and dear friends who come our way . . .

Let us honor perfect strangers,
And people of all nations,
Then with honor, peace on earth will come to stay!

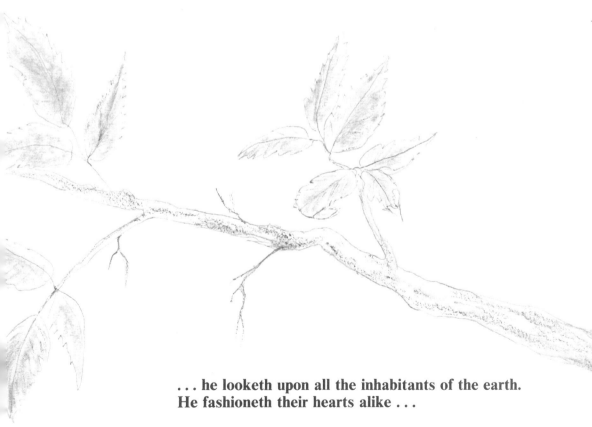

**. . . he looketh upon all the inhabitants of the earth.
He fashioneth their hearts alike . . .**

Psalms 33:14, 15

Patient Parent

We are all
God's children;
but only when we become
parents ourselves
do we realize
   how patient,
   how forgiving,
   how loving
     God is.

May we follow
His example
as we, too, hold our children
in the hollow of our hands.

Lo, children are an heritage of the Lord . . .

Psalms 127:3

Sabbath Feeling

There's a special feeling
That I get on Sabbath day,
As I join with all the others
And I meditate and pray,
And joyfully sing songs of praise
About Your loving way . . .
For, along with feeling peaceful,
And feeling rested, too,
A special feeling of renewal
Fills me through and through,
As I'm energized by all the love
Sent heaven bound to You!

Remember the sabbath day, to keep it holy.

Exodus 20:8

A Blessing for Baby

Bless me, Lord . . .
   I come into this great big world
   So helpless and so small,
   Yet I have a super power
   To bring joy and hope to all.

Guide me, Lord . . .
   Teach me ways in which to grow
   In soul as well as mind
   So everywhere I go I'll leave
   A touch of love behind.

Keep me, Lord . . .
   Hold me in Your loving arms
   Free from harm and strife,
   And let me feel Your presence near
   Through all days of my life.

Surely goodness and mercy shall follow me all the days of my life . . .

Psalms 23:6

Wee Treasure

The world's filled with wonderful things to behold,
Miracles, gifts of God's love—
The splendor of sunrise and sunsets of gold,
And galaxies twinkling above,
Summertime flowers, perfuming the air,
The softness of new-fallen snow,
Woods bursting with song and life everywhere,
And rainbows that set clouds aglow—
But, from all of these wonderful gifts, it is true
That nothing compares to the pleasure
Of having a baby, so dear and so new,
To cherish, to love, and to treasure!

Thy father and thy mother shall be glad, and she that bare thee shall rejoice.

Proverbs 23:25

Blessing for a Home

Bless this home and all within it,
Let it be a shelter for
Those who live here, friends who visit,
All who knock upon the door . . .

Bless this home with love and laughter,
Fill each room from wall to wall
With tenderness and understanding,
And peace within us one and all . . .

Bless this home and all within it,
Let it be a place to share
All the good gifts You have given,
Faith that's deep and earnest prayer!

Hear me, O Lord; for thy lovingkindness is good . . .

Psalms 69:16

A Thankful Gift

Bells are ringing, carolers singing,
Music fills the air,
Friends and families gather,
And love is everywhere . . .
It's a season filled with happiness,
With cheer and zestful living,
It's a season filled with meaning,
With closeness and with giving . . .
And I wonder, Lord, what kind of gift,
What can I give to You,
To half repay the gifts You give,
The wondrous things You do,
When all I have to offer
Has come from You above—
So, I'll give to You my service,
My thankful prayers . . . and love!

Serve the Lord with gladness . . .

Psalms 100:2

Wedding Vow

Two people have a special dream,
They're blessed by God above,
Their dream becomes reality,
They meet and fall in love . . .

Two hands are joined, a vow is said,
And two hearts beat as one,
And, with that vow, a whole new way
Of living has begun . . .

For there is no greater joy for two
Than that which comes from sharing—
No way to make life more complete
Than loving, giving . . . caring!

Two are better than one . . .

Ecclesiastes 4:9

Tapestry

Time has changed a lot of things,
But not the love we share,
For like a precious tapestry,
We've woven it with care . . .

Our tapestry is colored
With every kind of weather,
And bordered with the memories
Of times we've shared together . . .

It's patterned with a garden
Of dreams both old and new,
It has both thorns and roses,
Hopes dashed, and dreams come true . . .

And it will last eternally,
Our tapestry of love,
For we've woven in a golden thread
Of faith in God above!

My beloved is mine . . .

The Song of Solomon
2:16

Childhood Hopes and Dreams

A child's hopes are wonderful,
Unbound by fear or sorrow,
A child dares to scheme and dream
For every new tomorrow . . .

A child's faith is awesome,
It's accepting all there is
And knowing God is all things good—
And all good things are His . . .

A child's love is beautiful,
A warm and special glow,
That brings a touch of heaven
To everyone they know!

Be ye therefore followers of God, as dear children.

Ephesians 5:1

A Tribute to Mothers

A mother's arms are special.
From the start, they offer you
A place of warm security
You feel your whole life through . . .

A mother's eyes are special.
They have a tender way
Of looking for, and finding
The best in you each day . . .

A mother's heart is special,
Filled with sensitive emotion,
And wherever life will take you,
You will have her deep devotion . . .

A mother's faith is special,
And through it you will share
A closeness with the loving Lord
Who placed you in her care!

Her children arise up, and call her blessed . . .

Proverbs 31:28

Petition

Let me stay a little longer, Lord,
I've so much work to do,
And I need a bit more polish
Before I come to You . . .

Let me stay a wee bit longer, Lord,
There's so much left to see,
Let my eyes be open wider
Before You send for me . . .

Mind You, Lord, I'm not afraid
To come to You right now,
But I keep finding more to do
Right here on earth somehow . . .

In the middle of one dream, it seems,
A new goal fills my head.
There's so much left undone, Lord,
There's so much left unsaid . . .

The older that I get, I find
There's so much more to learn,
To fill my soul with yearning
And my heart with deep concern . . .

There are hungry people to be fed,
Heartaches to be cured,
Smiles to bring, roads to smooth,
And trials to be endured . . .

So, let me stay a little longer, Lord,
I've so much left to do.
I need to shine this soul of mine
Before I come to You!

They shall still bring forth fruit in old age . . .

Psalms 92:14

The Evening of Life

Softly, gently, holding me,
Enfolding me, lulling me,
My evening time is here . . .
My soul's at rest. My life's been blest,
For soon You will be calling me,
And, Lord, I have no fear.

I thank You, Lord, for faith, for love,
For blessings You have given,
For always being near . . .
And, most of all, I thank You
For your promise, Lord, of heaven
As my evening time is here.

His soul shall dwell at ease . . .

Psalms 25:13

Birthday Recipe

To give your day the proper start,
Wake up with a hopeful heart,
Then fill your day with things like these—
Friends, and fun, and memories.
Add some spice, a laugh or two,
Combine with favorite things to do,
Then to make it more delicious,
Add new dreams, new plans, and wishes,
Then top it with a mixture of
Sunshine, joy, and lots of love,
And birthday blessings from above!

Thou hast made known to me the ways of life; thou shalt make me full of joy with thy countenance.

Acts 2:28

Perspective

Each year
as we grow older,
we climb a little higher
toward the mountaintop of life . . .

and our
horizons broaden
with each step that takes us
higher toward the pinnacle of life.

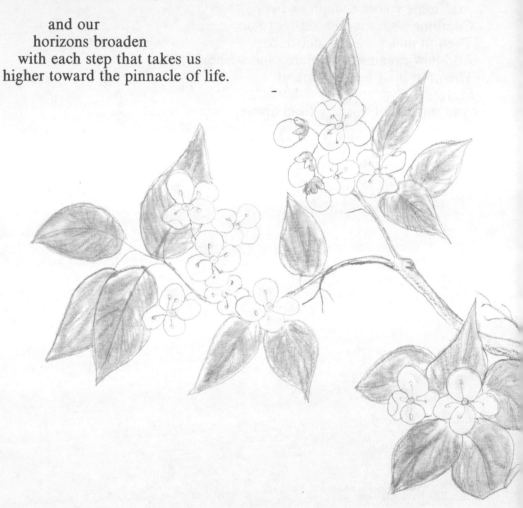

**Thou hast granted me life and favour, and thy visitation
hath preserved my spirit.**

Job 10:12

The Blessing of Friendship

What a blessing it is to have a dear friend
When life brings you sunshine and flowers,
Someone who helps make the most of good things
And who shares in your happiest hours!

What a comfort it is to have a dear friend
When a storm brews and cold winds are blowing,
Someone who's thoughtful, who holds out a hand,
Whose love and concern keep on showing!

What a treasure it is to have a dear friend
Through all times and all kinds of weather,
Someone to bear with, to care with, to share with ...
The blessings that life brings together!

Be kindly affectioned one to another ...

Romans 12:10

Beggar

Pardon me, Mister,
can you spare a smile?
I haven't had one
for such a long while.
It needn't be a big one,
any size will do to see me through
until tomorrow.
Thank you, Sir, and have a good day!

Excuse me, Ma'm,
Can I bother you for a kind word?
It seems ages since I heard
any sort of compliment.
It needn't be a big one,
a little bit of praise will get me through the day
until tomorrow.
Thank you, Ma'm, you have a lovely smile, too!

. . . he that is of a merry heart hath a continual feast.

Proverbs 15:15

Pass It On

She smiled
at a stranger in the elevator,
who, in turn,
passed it on to a salesclerk,
who then shared it with
another customer,
who brought it home
and gave it to her children,
who took it to school the next day
and multiplied it among
their friends and teachers.

Oh, what one little smile can do!

A merry heart maketh a cheerful countenance ...

Proverbs 15:13

Emma Lou

I visited a nursing home
To bring a bit of cheer,
To read some poems of faith and hope
And lend a listening ear.

I met a lot of people there
That cold day in December,
But there's one whose faith impressed me so,
I always will remember.

Emma Lou clomped down the stairs,
But what she lacked in grace
Was made up by the lovely smile
That shone upon her face.

She walked into the sitting room
And took her favorite chair,
Then greeted all the others
Who resided with her there.

She gently chided Nancy,
Who was sitting on the couch,
For feeling sorry for herself
And acting like a grouch.

Then Emma Lou took out the scarf,
Her knitting needles, too,
She lined the balls of yarn up—
The purple, mauve, and blue.

"Click, click," went her needles
As she spread her sunshine ways,
Dispelling gloom and darkness
Of her friends who shared her days.

I looked on with amazement
As she knitted row by row,
Counting blessings with her stitches,
Her countenance aglow . . .

For the nursing home I visited
Was a very special kind,
A home for sightless people,
And Emma Lou was blind.

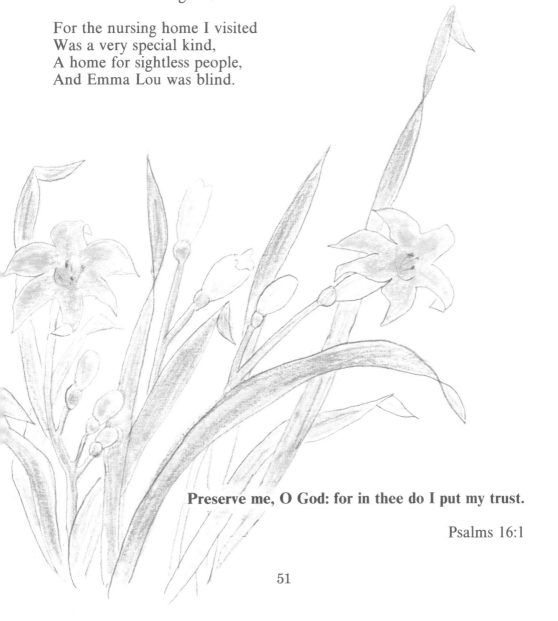

Preserve me, O God: for in thee do I put my trust.

Psalms 16:1

Remembering Grandma

Remembering . . .
    The warm and happy atmosphere
    That filled your home with warmth and cheer.

Remembering . . .
    The smiles, the tears, the hugs we shared,
    The many ways you showed you cared.

And though you're gone from earthly view,
These memories and others, too,
Still fill my thoughts, Grandma, of you!

**But thou, O Lord, shalt endure for ever; and
thy remembrance unto all generations.**

Psalms 102:12

3
Freedom and Peace

... With Love

"Let us love one another ..."
for with love
   comes understanding
and with understanding,
   everlasting peace.

. . . let us love one another . . . for God is love.

1 John 4:7, 8

Plowing Together

Let us plow the fields of mankind,
Let us plow the fields today.
Together, Lord, we'll lift out rocks
And break up clumps of clay . . .

We'll plant a seed of love that grows
Into a sturdy vine
Where tender blooms of peace,
And faith, and brotherhood entwine . . .

And from these blooms, new seeds will grow
Which we will hold in store
So the fields of mankind will know peace
And love forevermore!

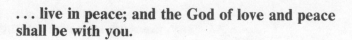

**. . . live in peace; and the God of love and peace
shall be with you.**

2 Corinthians 13:11

Freedom's Song

Down a shady country lane
And in a city street,
You see it in the eyes, Lord,
Of everyone you meet—
Freedom!

Living in a land like ours
Takes work and sacrifice,
Patience and forbearance—
But who can place a price
On Freedom!

In country lanes and city streets
The bells of hope are ringing—
Thank You, Lord, for giving us
This land where hearts are singing
Of Freedom!

Blessed is the nation whose God is the Lord; and the people whom he hath chosen for his own inheritance.

Psalms 33:12

Moving Mountains

Oh, we can move a mountain, Lord!
We'll move it stone by stone,
Faith will be our chisel
With strength from You alone . . .

We'll chip away at prejudice,
At ignorance and fear,
We'll bring Your words of brotherhood
To those who gather near . . .

Stone by stone, we'll move it,
This mountain made by hate,
Deed by deed and word by word,
Till it disintegrates . . .

Oh, we can move a mountain, Lord,
We'll do it stone by stone,
Till swords turn into plowshares
And peace and love are known!

. . . and they shall beat their swords into plowshares . . .

Isaiah 2:4

Three Wishes

Dear Lord,
If I had three wishes,
Three wishes You'd make good,
I'd wish for universal peace,
For love, and brotherhood.

If You'd only grant me two,
I'd wish for love and peace,
For, with enough of both of these,
All prejudice would cease.

If I had but one wish,
One gift from You above,
I'd fill the world with harmony
By wishing just for love!

These things I command you, that ye love one another.

John 15:17

Blessed Nation

Thank You, God, for this great nation,
A country with no parallel,
A melting pot of race and peoples,
A land where hope and freedom dwell ...

May we steer the way for others,
May we be a guiding force,
Bringing peace among all nations
With a sure and steady course ...

Thank You, God, for all our bounty,
Wealth enough to gladly share.
Thank You, God, for this great nation,
For Your guidance and Your care!

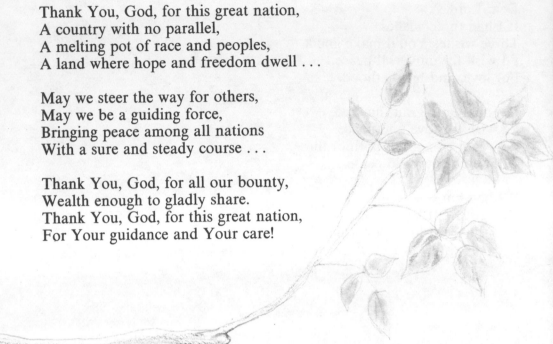

... the nations shall bless themselves in him ...

Jeremiah 4:2

Sharing in Peace

God gave to us, to everyone,
The twinkling stars, the warming sun,
God gave to you, God gave to me
The plains, the mountains, and the sea,
Fields to plow, blue skies above,
Friends to cherish and to love,
Birds, and flowers, changing seasons,
Dreams, desires, minds that reason,
Tender feelings, hearts that care—
God gave us all these things to share,
Wondrous gifts, so fine, so good,
To share in peace and brotherhood!

**Let us therefore follow after the
things which make for peace . . .**

Romans 14:19

4
Nature

Beauty

How does one find it,
   this wonder called beauty,
This marvel
   that poets extol?

The beauty of nature
   is found with the eyes,
The beauty of love
   with the soul!

. . . every perfect gift is from above . . .

James 1:17

60

Dame Nature's Answer

"Pardon me, Dame Nature,
I wonder if you mind
Giving me an answer
That is difficult to find.

All the seasons of the year
Have been so richly blessed,
Which one is your favorite,
Which do *you* love best?"

      "The budding hope of springtime,
      The softness of the snow,
      The fullness of the summer,
      And fall with leaves aglow . . .

      All of these were loving gifts
      From God who reigns above,
      So each are equal in my eyes
      And equal in my love!"

Thou crownest the year with thy goodness . . .

Psalms 65:11

Mystery

Invisible
hidden
out of sight
You do not show
Your face
yet
   every
      sunbeam
         dancing
reflects
Your golden grace!

. . . the earth is full of the goodness of the Lord.

Psalms 33:5

The Winter Is Past

When crocuses push through the snow,
When robins sing once more,
When new buds swell upon the trees,
And on the woodland floor,
When days begin to lengthen,
When sunshine warms the air,
Then springtime comes to tell us,
"God's love is everywhere!"

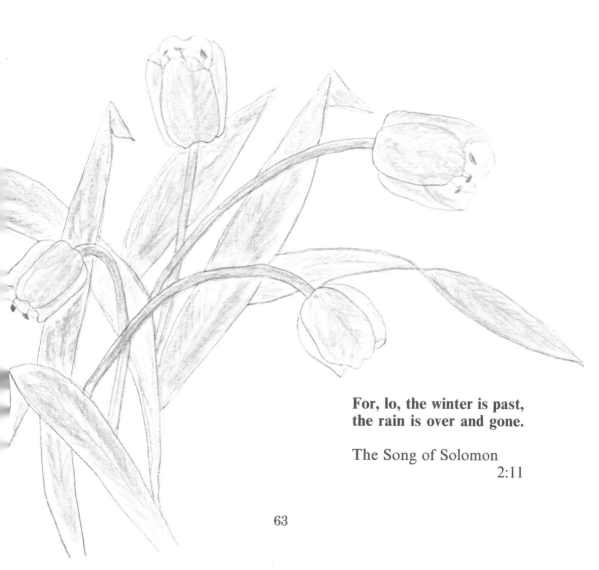

**For, lo, the winter is past,
the rain is over and gone.**

The Song of Solomon
2:11

The Woods Come Alive

Seeping
into the predawn sky
with the faintest blush,
almost shy, it came—
The birth of that first spring day.

Softly,
slowly, the sky melted to pink.
Then, with a secret cue,
the moisture left the air
leaving jewellike beads of dew
glistening everywhere.

Silently,
beneath the roots
of a sturdy tree
a mother rabbit nursed her brood,
while overhead three baby birds
waited openmouthed
for their hourly allotment of food.

Shining
ever brighter
the sun rose overhead,
loosening a last remnant of ice
from its sleepy winter bed, and sent
with bubbling merriment, a sliver of a stream
to find its way once more.

Pushing
their way through fallen leaves
new shoots carpeted the floor.
Sap flowed through the trees
and virgin buds perfumed the air.

Alive!
The woods came alive!
Alive for all to see
that life renews,
that life goes on
for all eternity!

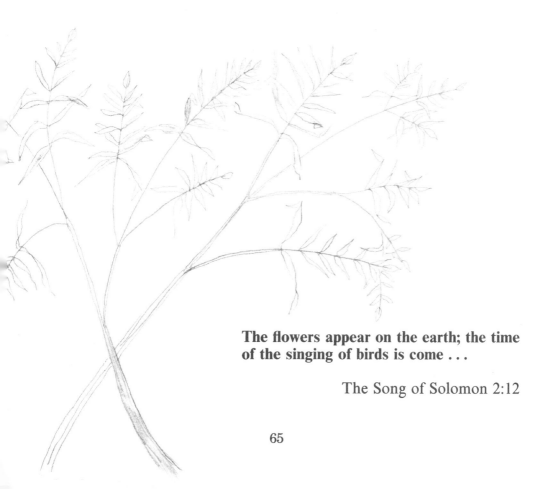

**The flowers appear on the earth; the time
of the singing of birds is come . . .**

The Song of Solomon 2:12

Gift Supreme

Through every season of the year
My heart, O Lord, is filled with praise,
A song of thanks for all the gifts
Brought forth from Your creative ways.
But especially now at springtime
When nature brings new life to be,
I'm thankful for the sacred gift—
Your promise of eternity!

**Thou sendest forth thy spirit, they are created:
and thou renewest the face of the earth.**

Psalms 104:30

Part of Thee

O Lord, who made the blazing stars,
And molecules too small to see,
Open up my mind to solve
A small part of Your mystery!

O Lord, who put the song in birds,
The thunderous roar into the sea,
Open up my ears to hear
A small part of Your melody!

O Lord, who brought forth life on earth
And lovingly created me,
Open up my soul to know
That I am but a part of Thee!

**Thou hast made known to me the ways of life; thou shalt
make me full of joy with thy countenance.**

Acts 2:28

Bountiful Blessings

Sunshine and showers, and colorful flowers,
Songbirds, and fruit-bearing trees,
Daily our lives are made richer
By wonderful things such as these . . .

Loved ones to care with, and dear friends to share with,
A storehouse of sweet memories,
Daily our lives are made brighter
By beautiful blessings like these . . .

As countless as stars up above us,
As countless as waves on the seas,
Your bountiful gifts are around us . . .
We thank You, dear Father, for these!

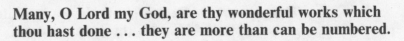

**Many, O Lord my God, are thy wonderful works which
thou hast done . . . they are more than can be numbered.**

Psalms 40:5

Like a Willow

Like a willow reaching down
to drink a summer shower,
I reach down with my soul roots
thirsting for an answer,
not certain of the question,
or what I'm searching for . . .

Like a flower reaching up
to feel the sun's warm rays,
I reach up with my spirit,
with a heartfelt prayer to You,
and a tender warmth enfolds me
as I feel Your love once more.

And the Lord God formed man of the dust of the ground . . .

Genesis 2:7

Majesty

You
whose might is displayed
in the roar of the sea,
the explosion of stars,
the splitting of atoms ...

You
whose love is shown
in the beauty of nature,
the cry of a newborn,
the promise of spring ...

You
whose face is hidden,
whose works are known,
whose name is uttered
in a thousand tongues ...

How can we praise You?
How can we know You?
How can we serve You?

We offer up our songs to praise You!
We offer up our hearts to know You!
We offer up our lives to serve You!

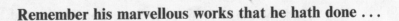

Remember his marvellous works that he hath done ...

Psalms 105:5

Snow Cathedral

Decorated in pure white
With crystal chandeliers,
Pillars reaching for the sky,
A holy atmosphere . . .

Music coming from an organ
Made of whistling winds—
A snow cathedral in the woods
Invites you to come in.

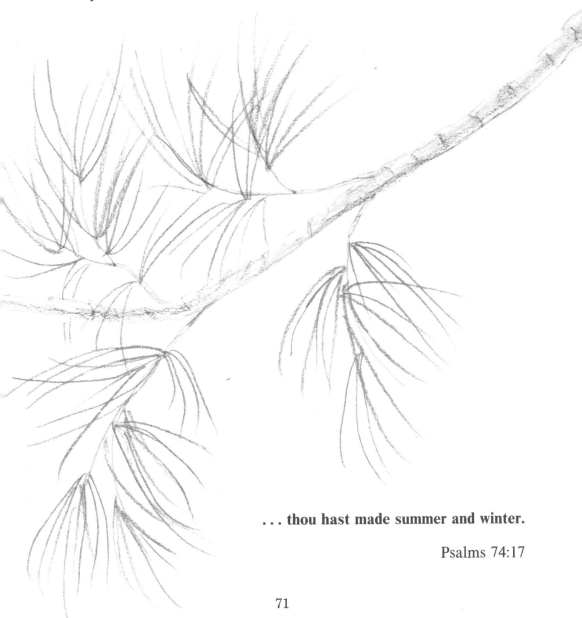

. . . thou hast made summer and winter.

Psalms 74:17

Everything That He Has Made

Robed in splendor nature stands
Displaying wonders of Your hands.

Crashing waves upon the shore,
Lightning and the thunder's roar,
Grazing beasts, and birds in flight
Tell of Your awesome will and might.

Rainbows after summer showers,
Fields of wheat and wild flowers,
Whispering winds, and shady trees,
Happy hours, sweet memories,
Work to do and goals to dare for,
Loved ones near to share and care for,
A finger clasped in baby's fist—
All these reveal You're in our midst!

And God saw every thing that he had made, and, behold, it was very good . . .

Genesis 1:31

God of All

O God of Awe,
God of All,
God of stars that shine,
Thank You for Your miracles,
And for this life of mine!

O God of all there was, there is,
And all You will to be,
Let my soul which You have made
Serve You eternally!

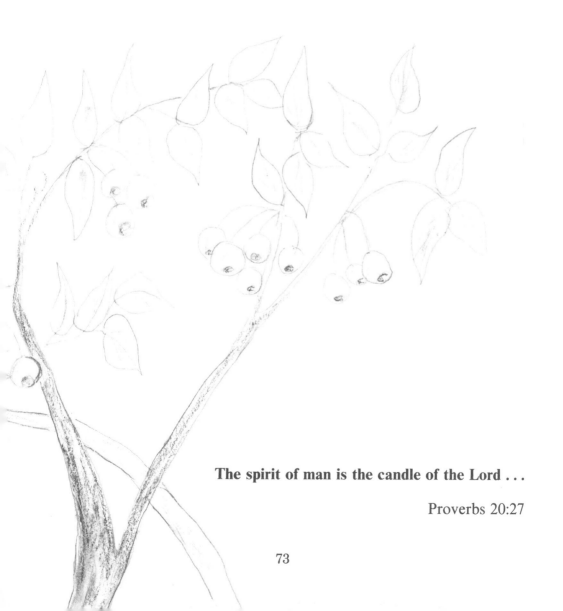

The spirit of man is the candle of the Lord . . .

Proverbs 20:27

Star Gazing

"Star light, star bright . . ."
A million stars
Lit up the night . . .

And childlike I gazed
And thought
How small I am,
And yet I, too,
Am part of all
The things God wrought!

The Lord that made the heaven and earth bless thee . . .

Psalms 134:3

Puppy Love

Pushed-in face,
  a wagging tail,
A bark that's still
  half whine, half wail,
Full of mischief,
  full of charm,
To hug and snuggle
  in your arms,
A fluffy, furry,
  fuzzy ball—
A God-made puppy—
  bless them all!

And God said, Let the earth bring forth
the living creature after his kind . . .

Genesis 1:24

Bouquet

One of
the most beautiful bouquets
I ever picked
was a memory bouquet
of a field of flowers
left untouched.

Help us to remember, Lord,
as we grow in might and power,
to leave a little space untouched
for growing wild flowers.

. . . every perfect gift is from above . . .

James 1:17

5
Faith

Spanning

Life is the span
between the everlasting   and the everlasting

and faith is the bridge
which holds it   all together.

For ever, O Lord, thy word is settled in heaven.

Psalms 119:89

What Is Faith?

Faith is
    a candle
    in the darkest dark . . .

    a harbor
    in a restless sea . . .

    a seed
    that blossoms in the sand. . . .

    the bond
    that binds myself to Thee!

. . . for the Lord preserveth the faithful . . .

Psalms 31:23

Wonderful Power

We all have our own
  special gifts we can use,
We all have our own
  destinations to choose,
Our own set of plans,
  of dreams to pursue,
Of goals to attain,
  of schemes to see through . . .

We can reach our desires,
  we can open doors wide,
With the wonderful power
  we all have inside,
For there's nothing on earth
  that you cannot achieve
With the power of faith
  when you truly believe!

**Ask, and it shall be given you;
seek, and ye shall find;
knock, and it shall be opened unto you.**

Matthew 7:7

Beacon

The journey through life has numerous roads,
New pathways to travel each day,
And with God there beside you, to keep you and guide you,
The journey is lighter some way . . .
So, wherever you wander, wherever you go,
Let faith be a beacon for you,
For the journey through life is sweet and complete
When the dear Lord is traveling with you!

. . . the Lord shall be unto thee an everlasting light . . .

Isaiah 60:19

Higher Still

We fly!
With man-made wings
and man-made fuel
we lift into the sky,
and with God's grace
we go beyond
to unknown realms
of stars and space . . .

And yet
we can fly higher still;
for with God's guidance
we can soar
on wings of faith
and bring to all
His love . . . His peace
forevermore!

**O Lord our Lord, how excellent is thy name in all the earth!
who hast set thy glory above the heavens.**

Psalms 8:1

Shifting Sands

The sands shift
to the rolling waves
that wash upon the shore,
and underneath
the shifting sands
exists the earth's firm core . . .

The sands of life
erode and shift
as time beats on the shore,
and firm beneath
is faith in God
and life forevermore.

Blessed is the man that trusteth in the Lord, and whose hope the Lord is.

Jeremiah 17:7

Walk My Way

Follow Me.
I will lead you
to the path
of perfect love

where joy and beauty
mingle,
where righteousness
reigns,
where light and truth
are one.

Walk My way
and I, the Hidden God,
will show Myself
to you.

Blessed are the pure in heart: for they shall see God.

Matthew 5:8

Truth

I am Truth,
born from the union
of Light and Wisdom.

I am old as time,
a friend of the prophets
and sages,
an enemy of evildoers,
darkness, and fear.

I have been used, abused,
ignored, abhorred, changed, rearranged,
and disdained.

My name has been
sanctified, beautified, hallowed,
blessed, and worshipped.

I am Truth
born from the union
of Light and Wisdom . . .
     a child of God.

Teach me thy way, O Lord; I will walk in thy truth . . .

Psalms 86:11

Honest Effort

Sometimes we're so afraid we'll fail,
We fail to even try.
We bury possibilities,
And let our efforts die . . .

We often don't remember
A fact that's widely known—
A mistake that brings a lesson
Is a handy stepping-stone . . .

So trust in God and trust yourself,
Don't be afraid to try
To broaden your horizon
And to reach up for the sky!

And I was afraid, and went and hid thy talent in the earth . . .

Matthew 25:25

A Blessed Place

Blessed is the place of worship
Where prayers come from the heart.

Blessed is the place of worship
Where acts of kindness start.

Blessed is the place of worship
Where teaching is a tool.

Blessed is the place of worship
Where the spirit of God rules.

Blessed is the place of worship
Where songs of praise are heard.

Blessed is the place of worship
That heeds God's every word.

Be it temple, church, or open field
With only sky above,
Blessed is the place of worship
That's filled with faith and love!

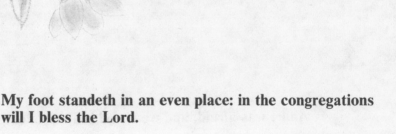

**My foot standeth in an even place: in the congregations
will I bless the Lord.**

Psalms 26:12

Trilogy

Your truth
is like a lamp to us.
We turn to it when shadows fall
And darkness comes our way.

Your love
is like a stove to us.
We welcome it into our hearts
to warm our lives each day.

Your promise
is a hope for us.
We feel it deep within our souls
each time we stop to pray!

For the Lord shall be thy confidence ...

Proverbs 3:26

The Sustainer

God is
the dawning
   of a bright new day,
sunlight streaming
   through a cloud,
springtime thawing
   winter's hold,
a shower falling
   on parched land.

God is
an anchor
   in a storm-tossed sea,
a rock
   to build a life on,
a beacon
   in a darkened world,
an ever-present
   helping hand.

**They that trust in the Lord shall be as mount Zion,
which cannot be removed, but abideth for ever.**

Psalms 125:1

Did You See God Today?

Did you see God today?
  "Yes, I did see God today!"
  A little child said,
  "I saw him in the pansy's face
  There in the garden bed!"

Did you see God today?
  "I looked into another's soul,"
  The poet spoke with care,
  "and I found hope, and faith, and love—
  I found God living there!"

Did you see God today?
  The scientist was cautious,
  But he, too, gave a nod,
  "I searched for explanations,
  For answers . . . and found God!"

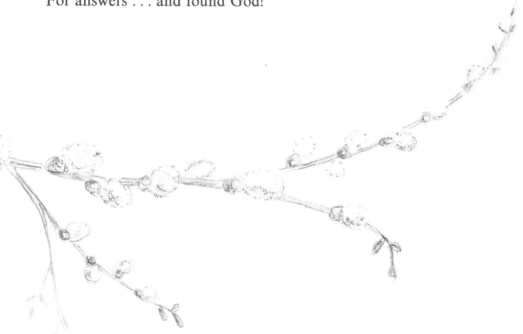

**Let every thing that hath breath praise the Lord.
Praise ye the Lord.**

Psalms 150:6

Great Mystery

Piece by piece,
generation by generation,
we unravel the great mysteries
of the universe.

Star by star,
galaxy by galaxy,
we discover the vastness
of creation.

Atom by atom,
molecule by molecule,
we search for the substance
of life.

And the more we learn,
the more we stand in awe
before the great mystery
of being.

**I am Alpha and Omega, the beginning and
the end, the first and the last.**

Revelation 22:13

Faith Upon Faith

With faith in God,
With faith in yourself,
    No hope is improbable,
    No dream is unattainable,
    No mountain insurmountable.

With faith in God,
With faith in yourself,
With faith upon faith,
    All things are possible.

. . . for with God all things are possible.

Mark 10:27

What More Could Any Father Do?

God gave us form and life and soul.
He made us with His love,
Then sent His rules for living
From a mountain high above . . .
  What more could any father do?

He soothes us and He calms us
When we're filled with fears and aches,
He guides us and forgives us
For our errors and mistakes . . .
  What more could any father do?

He lets us go out on our own
To win the things we yearn,
Yet His door is always open
And He welcomes our return . . .
  What more could any father do?

**Great is our Lord, and of great power:
his understanding is infinite.**

Psalms 147:5

Shining Through

Just as sunlight
finds its way
through heavy hanging boughs
to dance on woodland floors,
so, too, does faith shine through
our leaves of doubt
turning darkness into light,
sorrow into joy,
despair into hope.

Faith
is sunshine
heaven-sent
to light the paths
of mankind.

I am come a light into the world, that whosoever believeth on me should not abide in darkness.

John 12:46

6
Comfort

Hope for Tomorrow

Help me to remember, Lord,
When sadness comes my way
There's always a new tomorrow
To bring a brighter day . . .
And there's always some new blessing,
A lesson to learn, too,
When I have the faith to look ahead
Till tomorrow comes in view.

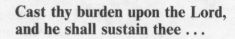

**Cast thy burden upon the Lord,
and he shall sustain thee . . .**

Psalms 55:22

Dawn Comes

Like a shroud,
a cloud of sorrow
clung to me.
Tears veiled the view
of my tomorrow
binding me.
Wrapped in a soft cocoon of pity,
I hung on,
waiting, wondering,
will I ever see the dawn?

"Help me, Lord,
see me through
this hurt and ache."

And with that anguished cry,
daylight began
to break!

**In the day when I cried thou answeredst me,
and strengthenedst me with strength in my soul.**

Psalms 138:3

Seek Out the Someone Who Loves You

When your burdens and cares seem more than your share,
When your heart's full of sorrow or grief,
Go seek out the Someone who loves you—
The One who will give you relief.

When you long for release, for comfort and peace,
When your vision is clouded by tears,
Go seek out the Someone who loves you—
The One who will calm all your fears.

You'll renew faith and hope, and be able to cope
With each problem, each sorrow, each care,
When you seek out the Someone who loves you—
When you go to the Lord with a prayer!

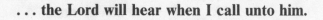

. . . the Lord will hear when I call unto him.

Psalms 4:3

Beyond Our Realm

Beyond the realm the living know
There lies a place of peace,
Where souls can find contentment
And joys that never cease.

In another realm of beauty,
Our loved ones go to share
The promise of eternity,
And meet our Father there.

And this is the promise that he hath promised us, even eternal life.

1 John 2:25

Eternal Light

A candle dims,
darkness comes,
a loved one leaves our sight,
gone beyond
to live again
in God's eternal light . . .

And, like the glow
a candle brings,
loving thoughts stay on,
with warm and special memories
to light the way
till dawn.

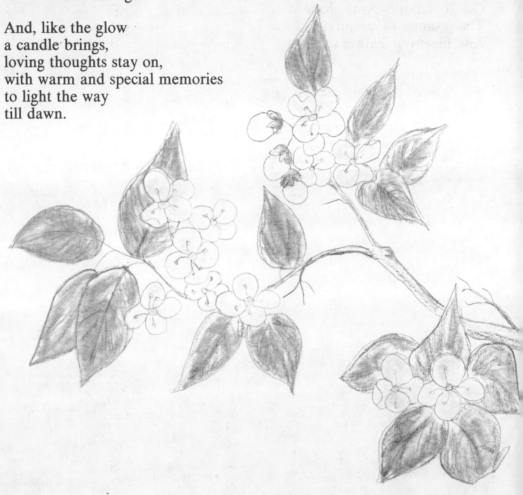

But thou, O Lord, shalt endure for ever; and thy remembrance unto all generations.

Psalms 102:12

Forever Friend

When the sea of life is stormy,
And the currents drag me under,
When the clouds shut out the sunlight,
And the air is thick with thunder,
I turn to You for guidance.
You give faith and hope to me.
You bring the sunlight out again.
You calm the stormy sea.

When the roads of life confuse me
And I can't see round the bend,
When I'm feeling lost and lonely
And I'm looking for a friend,
I turn to You for help again.
You light the way for me,
And I remember You're my friend
For all eternity!

**For thou wilt light my candle: the Lord my God
will enlighten my darkness.**

Psalms 18:28

Ever Near

Remember there is Someone
Ever present, ever near,
Someone who adores you
And holds you very dear . . .

When you need His help, just reach out
He will take you by the hand,
He will comfort you and guide you,
He will help you understand . . .

He will give you strength and courage,
To cast out doubt and fear—
Remember there is Someone
Ever present, ever near.

. . . perfect love casteth out fear . . .

1 John 4:18

Be Not Afraid

Sometimes the clouds hang heavy,
The sunlight seems shut out,
Sometimes the world looks dark for you,
Your mind is full of doubt—
Keep your faith and go to God
To cast your worries out . . .

Sometimes life's road is rocky
And the hills seem high for you,
Sometimes the way is lonely
And fearful for you, too—
Be not afraid, only believe,
God is there with you.

. . . **Be not afraid, only believe.**

Mark 5:36

Guidance

Walking round and round in circles,
Knowing not which way to turn,
Filled with fear and indecision,
Where to go in life's sojourn . . .
I stopped and gazed upon the maze
Of crossroads everywhere,
And as I stopped, I looked within
While uttering a prayer . . .
As I prayed for help and guidance,
A small still voice came through,
"Have faith and fear not, child,
I will light the way for you!"

**My help cometh from the Lord, which made
heaven and earth.**

Psalms 121:2

Tomorrow

Be with me, Lord, tomorrow,
And still my trembling heart,
Be with me, Lord, tomorrow,
As I make a brand-new start . . .

Walk beside me, Lord, and guide me
As I walk an unknown road,
Give me fortitude to climb the hills,
And strength for any load . . .

Be with me, Lord, tomorrow,
And the days that follow, too,
Let my success be Our success
In everything We do!

**My soul waiteth for the Lord more than they
that watch for the morning . . .**

Psalms 130:6

Looking Ahead

Looking out on barren fields,
On clumps of frozen soil,
The farmer sits preparing
For his yearly springtime toil . . .

In catalogs he reads about
The latest tools and seeds,
Reflecting on his blessings,
And the hungry his land feeds . . .

So, too, when "winter" comes our way
And hopes seem dashed or dead,
With faith we must look forward
Knowing "spring" is just ahead!

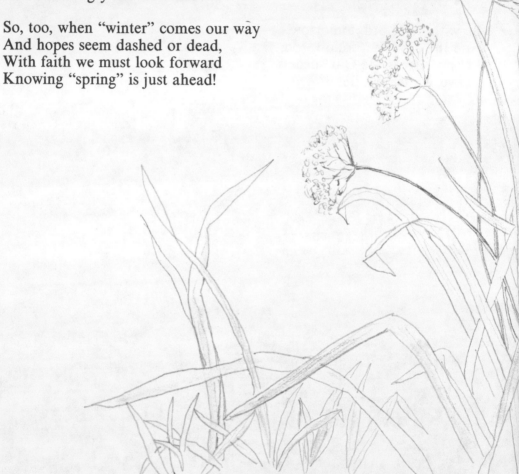

**I will lift up mine eyes unto the hills,
from whence cometh my help.**

Psalms 121:1

Cast Your Cares

It's not a pretty package, Lord,
We send to You in prayer—
Anxieties and worries
All wrapped up in despair . . .

We cast out all our troubles,
Our cares and woeful things,
And You receive them as a gift
A little child brings . . .

And in exchange You give us peace,
And strength and hope anew—
How boundless is Your care for us,
How great Your love is, too!

Casting all your care upon him; for he careth for you.

1 Peter 5:7

Growing Stronger

God gives us
little burdens to carry
so that we may gain strength
to handle the big ones . . .

And when we have mastered those,
we will be strong enough
to reach out a helping hand
to others.

But they that wait upon the Lord shall renew their strength . . .

Isaiah 40:31

The Promise Fulfilled

The searing heart-hurt of a loss—
How can we bear the pain,
Knowing that we'll never see
A loved one once again?

But, wait, let's still our tears in prayer
And listen to the Lord,
"Grieve not, your loved one's come to claim
A heavenly reward.
Remember that I promised
If you believe in Me,
Salvation of the soul is yours
For all eternity!"

The tears subside, the heart-hurt quells,
And we can bear the pain,
Knowing that someday we'll see
Our loved ones once again.

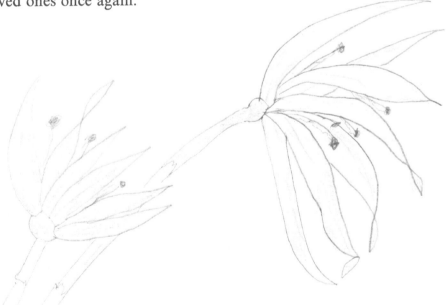

Out of the depths have I cried unto thee, O Lord.

Psalms 130:1

7
Prayer

Soul Song

Prayer
is the soul song
God hears
even before
the notes
are written.

**Thou knowest my downsitting and mine uprising,
thou understandest my thought afar off.**

Psalms 139:2

Too Busy to Pray

There's so much to do,
New feats to be won,
My shoulders are small
For the tasks to be done.
(I'm too busy today
To take time to pray.)

There are problems to solve
To add to my load,
As I stumble along
down life's rocky road.
(I'm too tired today
To take time to pray.)

My faith's running low,
I've enough grief and sorrows
To fill up today
And all my tomorrows!
(I just wish I could find
Some peace for my mind.
If I only could spare
A brief moment for prayer . . .)

God is our refuge and strength, a very present help in trouble.

Psalms 46:1

Morning Prayer

Help me, Heavenly Father,
As I start a brand-new day,
To meet whatever challenges
Life may bring my way . . .
Let me temper all my judgments
With love and understanding,
Teach me to be patient
And a little less demanding . . .
Grant me courage as I need it
For unfamiliar roads,
And strength enough to carry
The heaviest of loads . . .
Guide me, Heavenly Father,
And make me worthy of
This brand-new day You've given me,
And bless me with Your love.

. . . when I awake, I am still with thee.

Psalms 139:18

New Year Prayer

Put Your hand upon my shoulder,
Let me feel Your presence near,
Stay close to me and guide me
As I start another year . . .

Let my efforts all be fruitful,
Let my thoughts and little deeds
Grow into something beautiful
From faith-filled fertile seeds . . .

Let me be Your humble servant,
Serving You and You alone,
Let my acts reflect Your goodness
And all the love You've shown!

**Commit thy way unto the Lord; trust also in him;
and he shall bring it to pass.**

Psalms 37:5

Open Gates and Open Doors

The gates of prayer
   are always open
      and all who enter there
Will find sweet solace,
   perfect peace, and answers
      to their every care.

      The doorways
         to His house are many
            different tongues and different creeds
      But once inside
         we all remember
            all of us are of one seed.

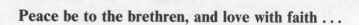

Peace be to the brethren, and love with faith ...

Ephesians 6:23

Supplication

Here I am again, Lord,
Asking You for more,
When I can't even start to count
The things I'm thankful for . . .
But like a patient parent,
Your well of love is deep,
You fill my needs when I'm awake,
And guard me when I sleep . . .
So hear my supplication,
But know it's bringing, too,
My deepest love and gratitude
For everything You do!

**For thou, Lord, art good, and ready to forgive; and
plenteous in mercy unto all them that call upon thee.**

Psalms 86:5

Making Contact

Let me touch one life today,
Let my hands reach out
And bring a ray of hope and faith
To someone who's in doubt . . .

Let me touch one life today,
One fellow human being
Who might be blind with prejudice
And needs my eyes for seeing . . .

Let me touch one life today,
And help a hurting heart
See the sunshine through the clouds
And make a brand-new start . . .

With understanding words or deeds,
Or with a simple task,
Let me touch one life today—
One life—that's all I ask!

. . . let us not love in word, neither in tongue;
but in deed and in truth.

1 John 3:18

Praise With Harp

Let my voice become a harp, Lord,
So when my prayer comes through,
My praise will be as sweet
As all the gifts I get from You . . .

Let my hands become a chapel
As I send my thoughts above,
Let my heart become a vessel
Brimming o'er with faith and love . . .

Let my voice become a harp, Lord,
Plucking out a song of praise
Singing sweetly, oh, so sweetly
Of Your gifts that fill my days!

. . . praise him with the psaltery and harp.

Psalms 150:3

8
Through the Year

A special collection of prayer poems
for every month of the year.

Another Year, Another Chance

Thank You, Father, thank You,
For this year fresh and new,
Another chance to know Your love—
To show my love for You . . .

Another chance to make amends
For yesteryear's mistakes,
To ask forgiveness and forgive
Those little hurts and aches . . .

Thank You for this day that brings
New dreams, new plans, new hopes,
Along with all the strength I need
To climb the steepest slopes . . .

Thank You, Father, thank You,
For this day so fresh and new,
A chance to grow, a chance to show
My boundless love for You!

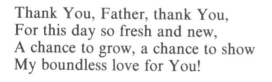

**Every day will I bless thee; and I will praise
thy name for ever and ever.**

Psalms 145:2

Loveshine

Dear Lord,
I get a sunny kind of feeling
When Your loveshine warms my heart—
My troubles turn to bubbles
And my fears and doubts depart . . .

Thank You for that feeling,
That warm and special glow—
I pray that I can pass it on
To everyone I know . . .

Please use me as a ray, Dear Lord,
To make each day much brighter,
By word or deed to fill a need
And make a burden lighter . . .

And let me use Your loveshine
In everything I do,
That in a humble way I'll be
A mirror, Lord, of You!

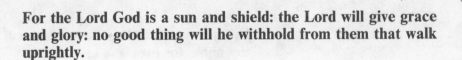

**For the Lord God is a sun and shield: the Lord will give grace
and glory: no good thing will he withhold from them that walk
uprightly.**

Psalms 84:11

Breezes, Winds, and Hurricanes

For howling winds
That make me bend,
And make me stronger
In the end,
I thank You, Lord!

For hurricanes
That tear at roots,
Forcing me
to grow new shoots,
I thank You, Lord!

For winds of love,
I thank You, Lord,
The soothing breeze
Of faith's reward,
I thank You, Lord!

God is our refuge and strength, a very present help in trouble.

Psalms 46:1

Rebirth

I'm singing, Lord, I'm singing
A soul-song filled with praise
As with a soft and gentle touch,
You bring on springtime days!

I'm singing, Lord, I'm singing
A song of thanks to You,
Renewing life around me,
The spirit in me too!

Glory hallelujah
To He who dwells on high
Who made the changing seasons,
The sea, the sod, the sky!

Thank You for the miracles
That springtime brings to earth,
For life that's everlasting,
And for my soul's rebirth!

Thou wilt shew me the path of life: in thy presence is fulness of joy; at thy right hand there are pleasures for evermore.

Psalms 16:11

Meditation on a Rose

The rose is nature's gift of love,
And as I watch it bloom,
I marvel at the sweetness
Of its delicate perfume.

My heart is filled with praise, Lord,
For this very special gift,
And the lesson that it teaches
When my spirit needs a lift . . .

It's a lesson that in spite of thorns,
The painful barbs of strife,
My faith can bloom as sweetly
Above the trials of life.

**Be pleased, O Lord, to deliver me: O Lord,
make haste to help me.**

Psalms 40:13

Quiet Moments

Thank You, Lord, for quiet moments,
Little "Sabbaths" in the day,
For the feeling of contentment
When I meditate and pray . . .

Thank You, Lord, for Your commandments,
Words to take me down life's roads,
Words of wisdom, words of guidance,
Words that lighten all my loads . . .

Thank You, Lord, for stars to reach for,
Plans and goals I'm dreaming of,
Thank You, Lord, for quiet moments
When I know Your peace and love!

Blessed be the Lord, because he hath heard the voice of my supplications.

Psalms 28:6

A Step Toward Peace

You gave us
    messages of peace
        and we ignored them.
You sent us
    messengers of peace
        and we deplored them.

Now we come before You, Lord . . .

Help me take
    one small step
        toward understanding others.
Help me, Lord,
    to realize
        that all men are my brothers!

I will hear what God the Lord will speak:
for he will speak peace unto his people . . .

Psalms 85:8

Beautiful People

Loving parents,
  giving, caring,
Special friends
  for fun and sharing,
Teachers
  widening our view,
Clergy
  guiding me to You.
Thank You, Lord,
  for all and each.
Let my life
  fulfill their reach.

For thou, Lord, wilt bless the righteous ...

Psalms 5:12

Supreme Power

Give me, give me, give me!
  Position, rank, and power . . .
The hunger, Lord, for things
  Can fill our waking hours.

I'm well aware, Dear Father,
  I catch the fever too,
I concentrate too much on things
  And not enough on You.

But when I pause to meditate
  On what means most to me,
YOU are my mind's contentment,
  My soul's tranquility.

**O Lord, thou hast searched me, and known me.
Thou knowest my downsitting and mine uprising,
thou understandest my thought afar off.**

Psalms 139:1, 2

Daily Benefit

For answering so many prayers,
For helping me through trials and cares,
I thank You!

For dreams to dream, for plans to make,
For brand-new goals to undertake,
I thank You!

For giving me the zest and will
To keep me reaching higher still,
I thank You, Lord, I thank You!

Blessed be the Lord, who daily loadeth us with benefits . . .

Psalms 68:19

Good Harvest

My heart is filled with thanks, Lord,
For the harvest You bestow,
Not only for the grains and fruits
That You have caused to grow,
But for the harvest of the soul,
The good things that I feel,
The closeness of my family,
The friendships that are real . . .
And thank You, Lord, for planting
These seeds within me too,
A thirst for knowledge, cherished dreams,
A faith that's deep and true.

**Let us come before his presence with thanksgiving,
and make a joyful noise unto him with psalms.**

Psalms 95:2

The Prince of Peace

Praise to You, O Holy One,
Source of our salvation,
For out of darkness You brought light
That first day of creation . . .

And when the world went dark again
And evil walked the earth,
You sent a Guiding Light to us,
O praise His Holy Birth . . .

He leads us out of darkness
He gives new hope to men—
O praise His Name, His Holy Name
As Christmas comes again!

**Light is sown for the righteous, and gladness
for the upright in heart.**

Psalms 97:11